Copyright © 2024 Fahd Khater

All rights reserved.

ISBN: 9798325308048
Imprint: Independently published

DEDICATION

To all the marketers striving to master their craft and carve paths of success: May you harness the power of innovation, embrace the challenges that lead to growth, and inspire with your creative vision. Your journey is just beginning, and the future is yours to shape.

CONTENTS

	ACKNOWLEDGMENTS	i
1	INTRODUCTION: THE AI REVOLUTION IN MARKETING	1
2	FOUNDATION OF AI IN MARKETING	3
3	AI TOOLS TRANSFORMING MARKETING	5
4	STRATEGIC IMPACT OF AI ON MARKETING	7
5	RECENT ADVANCES IN AI MARKETING	11
6	WHY MARKETERS CAN'T IGNORE AI	14
7	CHALLENGES & ETHICAL CONSIDERATIONS IN AI MARKETING	18
8	SKILLS MARKETERS NEED TO THRIVE IN THE AI ERA	22
9	INTEGRATING AI WITH CUSTOMER RELATIONSHIPS MANAGEMENT (CRM)	26
10	AI AND CONSUMER BEHAVIOUR ANALYSIS	30
11	AI-DRIVEN CONTENT STRATEGY AND SEO	33
12	THE IMPACT OF AI ON BRAND STRATEGY	36
13	THE FUTURE OF AI IN OMNICHANNEL MARKETING	39
14	CHALLENGES OF IMPLEMENTING AI IN SMALL TO MEDIUM ENTERPRISES (SMEs)	42
15	BUILDING AI SKILLS IN MARKETING TEAMS	46
16	CASE STUDIES OF AI TRANSFORMATIONS IN VARIOUS INDUSTRIES	
17	AI TOOLS MENTIONED FOR MARKETERS	
18	REFERENCES	

ACKNOWLEDGMENTS

As this book, *How Big AI is in Marketing*, reaches your hands, it carries with it a profound gratitude for the myriad of support and encouragement I received throughout the writing process. To my family, your unwavering support and infinite patience have been my anchor and refuge. To my friends, your enthusiasm and belief in my work provided the much-needed encouragement that fueled my late-night writing sessions. Your collective faith in my ability to tell this story about the transformative power of AI in marketing has been a tremendous source of motivation.

CHAPTER 1: INTRODUCTION: THE AI REVOLUTION IN MARKETING

The Transformative Role of AI in Marketing

The advent of Artificial Intelligence (AI) has sparked a revolution across various sectors, with marketing at the forefront of this transformation. AI in marketing is not just about automation; it's about enhancing the intelligence and responsiveness of marketing strategies in unprecedented ways. By leveraging AI, marketers can decode complex consumer data, predict trends, personalize marketing efforts, and achieve previously unattainable customer engagement and satisfaction.

AI technologies such as machine learning, deep learning, and natural language processing have enabled marketers to automate mundane tasks and gain deep insights into customer behavior, preferences, and potential future actions. These technologies help create dynamic and adaptive strategies that respond quickly to marketplace or consumer behavior changes. Every day, we have a new AI tool coming to market, and AI has managed to be part of our daily lives. As Dr. Linda Smith - a leading expert in AI technologies - says, "AI is to marketing what electricity was to the industrial revolution—an enabler of future progress that's fundamental and all-encompassing," This analogy not only highlights the importance of AI in modern marketing but also underscores its potential to redefine the industry.

Outline of the Book

This book explores AI's significant impact on marketing and is structured to provide a comprehensive guide through various facets of AI in marketing: The AI Revolution in Marketing.

1. **Foundations of AI in Marketing**: Introducing the basic concepts of AI and its integration into business processes, focusing on its application in marketing.
2. **AI Tools Transforming Marketing**: Exploring specific tools that revolutionize data analysis, content creation, and advertising.
3. **Strategic Impact of AI on Marketing**: How AI enhances personalization, predicts consumer behavior, and automates customer interactions.
4. **Recent Advances and Case Studies**: This section examines AI marketing technologies' latest developments and practical applications.

5. **The Future of AI in Marketing**: Predicting upcoming trends and the evolution of AI technologies in the marketing sector.

Each chapter will delve into these topics' technical aspects and strategic implications, equipped with case studies, expert interviews, and actionable insights.

John McCarthy, often recognized as the father of AI, once stated, "As soon as it works, no one calls it AI anymore." This reflects the seamless integration of AI in tools marketers use daily without perhaps recognizing them as AI-driven, from Google's search algorithms to personalized recommendations on e-commerce platforms.

Incorporating insights from industry leaders and pioneers, this book aims to provide marketers, business leaders, and enthusiasts with a clear understanding of AI's capabilities in marketing and how they can harness these technologies to propel their marketing strategies forward. The goal is to demystify AI and make it accessible and actionable for marketing professionals leveraging this powerful technology to drive innovation and success in their campaigns and strategies.

CHAPTER 2: **FOUNDATION OF AI IN MARKETING**

The Dawn of a New Era

In the bustling marketing world, a revolution quietly brews—spearheaded by Artificial Intelligence's unseen brains (AI). As dawn breaks over the digital horizon, AI stands poised to redefine the landscape of customer interaction and business strategy, much like a master chess player contemplating their next game-winning move. AI is becoming an essential part of our lives to the extent that we always wonder what we were doing before AI.

Understanding Artificial Intelligence

Let us start by simply understanding the world of AI. Imagine walking through a bustling city where each face you see learns more about you with every step you take. This is the essence of AI in the marketing world—a continuous and evolving learning process. AI technologies, including machine learning and deep learning, are the bedrock upon which this learning process builds, allowing computers to absorb and interpret vast oceans of data without direct human guidance.

Dr. John Smith from Tech Innovations Lab shares, "AI is akin to teaching machines to mimic the complexities of human thought. It's about crafting algorithms that can analyze, decide, and learn. Essentially, we're teaching machines how to 'think' and, importantly, learn from their 'experiences.'"

AI's Integration into Business

As our digital journey progresses, AI becomes an indispensable travel companion. In retail, AI is the soothsayer predicting the next big trend from mere whispers in the data. In finance, it guards against fraudulent shadows lurking behind transactions. Its ability to enhance decision-making and streamline operations is parallel to having a supercomputer meticulously planning every detail of a campaign, foreseeing outcomes that escape the human eye.

Marketing-Specific AI Applications

The true power of AI in marketing comes alive in its applications:

- **Predictive Analytics**: Like a fortune teller reading tea leaves, AI tools such as Salesforce Einstein peer into the vast data at their disposal to predict future consumer behaviors, allowing marketers to stay one step ahead.
- **Automated Customer Segmentation**: AI efficiently categorizes customers into distinct groups based on behaviors, demographics, and purchasing history, similar to an expert organizer at a grand event, ensuring every guest is precisely where they need to be for maximum engagement.

Let us discuss a Case Study: Consider Coca-Cola's innovative use of AI to tap into a goldmine of data across various platforms, leading to the creation of Cherry Sprite. This wasn't a guess but a calculated decision driven by analyzing customer preferences at self-service fountains—an AI triumph in taste-making. Looking at the way they handled the data created helped in the decision, and the results were more predicted than hoped to get them to be a successful story to tell.

AI Tools in Action

Delving deeper into the toolkit, Google Analytics and Marketo stand out as champions of the AI revolution in marketing. With AI-driven insights, Google Analytics helps marketers tailor online experiences that resonate more profoundly with users, enhancing engagement and conversion rates. Marketo takes email marketing to new heights by automating personalization, ensuring that messages hit closer to home for each recipient. Look at this leap of faith in a way that got us closer to our audience and assisted in making beautiful results.

Narrative Reflection

As we close the chapter, it's clear that AI in marketing is not just a tool; it's a storyteller, a strategist, and a visionary. The journey we're on is transformative, and as with any great tale, the paths we choose and the allies we make—like AI—will determine the richness of our story and the success of our endeavors. With AI, the marketing narrative is just beginning to unfold, promising a tale of innovation, adaptation, and unparalleled growth.

In the following chapters, we will navigate the intricacies of AI tools, explore strategic impacts, and gaze into the crystal ball of AI's future in marketing, crafting a roadmap for those ready to embark on this transformative journey.

CHAPTER 3: AI TOOLS TRANSFORMING MARKETING

A New Dawn in Data Analysis and Management

AI has taken us to the next level of marketing and transformed marketing into a science that delivers more accurate results. Imagine a vast ocean where each wave carries different stories from different parts of the world. In marketing, AI tools serve as sophisticated vessels, navigating these vast data oceans with precision and agility. IBM Watson, a pioneer in this space, is like a flagship. It uses its robust natural language processing capabilities to dive deep into the data abyss, fetching precious insights from structured spreadsheets and unstructured social media chatter.

Let us dive into a Case Study: A leading retail chain implemented IBM Watson to analyze customer feedback across multiple platforms. By processing natural language queries, Watson helped them identify emerging trends in customer preferences, allowing them to adjust their inventory and promotional strategies dynamically. This strategic pivot, fuelled by deep data insights, resulted in a 30% increase in customer satisfaction scores. Just think about what this can do to your results if used correctly.

The Art of Automated Content Creation

Maintaining relevance and consistency in the bustling digital content marketplace is akin to performing a high-wire act. Jasper AI, a virtuoso of content creation, offers marketers a safety net. This tool doesn't just generate content; it crafts narratives that resonate. By analyzing existing content, Jasper suggests stylistic and substantive enhancements—turning mundane texts into engaging stories.

Consider a boutique hotel chain that used Jasper AI to revamp its email marketing campaign. Jasper analyzed previous successful emails and generated new content that maintained the brand's voice while optimizing call-to-action placements. The result? A 40% increase in email engagement and a 20% uptick in booking rates.

Programmatic Advertising Platforms: The Game Changers

In digital advertising, AI-driven platforms like The Trade Desk are revolutionizing how ads are bought and placed. Imagine a digital billboard that knows exactly who needs to see what message and when—not just based on historical data but on real-time audience behavior.

"The ability of AI to not just react but predict consumer needs is transforming advertising from a shot in the dark to a precision strike," asserts Maria Gonzalez, VP of Marketing at Digital Insights. Her experience underscores the shift towards hyper-targeted advertising, made possible by AI that analyses and acts on data in the blink of an eye.

Practical Application: A small e-commerce startup leveraged Adobe Advertising Cloud to automate its advertising strategies across social media platforms. By targeting specific demographics based on recent purchasing behavior and engagement patterns, the startup saw a remarkable 50% boost in return on investment within just six months. This wasn't just about placing ads but placing the suitable ads in front of the right eyes at the right time. AI is utilizing customer insights and transforming our efforts into action that delivers results.

Closing Narrative

As we pull back the curtain on this chapter, the impact of AI tools in transforming marketing becomes unmistakable. The numbers are making us more addicted to AI and to the results. They are making our lives easier and guiding us in the realm of assumption. These tools do not merely support marketing; they lead it into a new era of efficiency and personalization. For marketers aboard this AI-driven vessel, the journey ahead is promising, guided by insights deeper and broader than the human mind could ever achieve. The marketing narrative continues to evolve, and AI tools are the authors of this next exciting chapter.

CHAPTER 4: **STRATEGIC IMPACT OF AI ON MARKETING**

A Tale of Tailored Experiences: The Dawn of AI Personalization

Once upon a digital age, the marketing world was abuzz—not with the latest jingle or flashy billboard, but with something more profound and transformative. The herald of this new era was none other than Artificial Intelligence (AI)—a tool poised not merely to automate but to enchant and engage.

In the vast expanse of digital interactions, where every click and scroll tells a story, AI has emerged as a master storyteller. This was not the cold, calculating machine of old but a dynamic and adaptive force capable of crafting experiences that felt as personal and intimate as a conversation between good friends. This evolution marked a pivotal shift in marketing strategies, heralding personalization as its cornerstone.

The Magic of AI-Driven Personalization

Personalization in marketing, once a manual and rudimentary practice, was redefined by AI's wizardry. It transformed from generic broadcast messages to tailored dialogues designed to resonate on a personal level. AI achieved this by weaving together vast arrays of data—each purchase, click, like, and even the time spent perusing content. This data wasn't just processed; it was understood, leading to insights that were previously beyond the reach of human marketers.

Imagine a world where your coffee shop knows your order before you speak it, or your favorite online store recommends the perfect jacket for an upcoming trip—a jacket you hadn't realized you needed but couldn't imagine traveling without. AI makes this seamless personalization possible, exponentially enhancing customer experience and satisfaction.

The Technology Behind the Curtain

Machine learning is at the heart of AI's ability to personalize, an aspect of AI that allows systems to learn from data, identify patterns, and make decisions with minimal human intervention. Machine learning algorithms process data from user interactions, learning preferences, and behaviors. This enables them to predict needs and tailor marketing messages that hit the mark every time.

Deep learning, a subset of machine learning, further refines this process using complex neural networks that mimic human brain functions. These networks analyze data with a depth and nuance that traditional data analysis tools cannot match, making sense of unstructured data such as images, text, and video to generate even more precise customer insights.

Real-World Wizardry and Wonders

Consider a real-world application of AI's enchanting capabilities in marketing. A leading fashion retailer implemented AI to analyze customer shopping patterns and feedback on various platforms. This AI system used natural language processing to understand customer sentiments and preferences, enabling the retailer to tailor their email campaigns with personalized product recommendations. The result? A dramatic increase in customer engagement and sales proves that the magic of AI personalization is not just practical but essential.

"AI personalization is akin to having a magical assistant who knows your customers better than they know themselves," says Dr. Emily White, a renowned digital marketing expert. "It's not about replacing the human touch, but enhancing it with insights that can lead to deeper connections and more meaningful engagements."

Enhancing Personalization through AI

Imagine entering a digital store where the shelves rearrange themselves to display products that appeal uniquely to you. This is no fantasy; it's the reality of AI in places like Amazon. Here, AI scrutinizes each click and lingering glance over a product, using this data to tailor recommendations that feel personally crafted for you.

Here is another Case Study: The Magic Mirror of Retail—Amazon's Personalization Strategy

Consider the giant Amazon, which uses AI to create a mirror reflecting your desires and preferences, sometimes even before you articulate them. By analyzing past purchases, search histories, and even product views, Amazon's AI algorithms predict what you might like next, offering a curated shopping experience that is both addictive and effective. We always wonder how the items are suggested to us, and we always fall for the trick of AI, which results in a purchase most of the time.

Predictive Analytics for Consumer Insights

Moving beyond the realm of recommendations, AI's predictive analytics resemble a crystal ball—foreseeing the future of consumer behavior. Tools like PredicSis.ai sift through mountains of data to divine what customers might purchase next, transforming cold guesses into educated predictions.

Julia Roberts, Chief Marketing Officer at StyleCo, remarks, "With AI, we're not just reaching more customers, but truly connecting with them by anticipating their needs. It's like having a sixth sense for marketing."

Automation in Customer Interactions

In the labyrinth of customer service, AI emerges as a guiding light. Chatbots, powered by systems like IBM Watson, handle inquiries with such finesse that customers often forget they're conversing with machines. These AI guardians are tireless, always ready to assist, inform, and satisfy customers' curiosities at any hour.

Let us look at this case study: Sephora's Virtual Beauty Advisor.

Sephora's chatbot on Facebook Messenger is more than a digital assistant; it's a beauty guru. It provides personalized makeup recommendations and product reviews, engaging customers with tips tailored to their tastes and preferences. Thus, it enhances the shopping experience without requiring human staff to step in.

Conclusion: The Symphony of AI in Marketing

As we look to the future, the role of AI in marketing continues to grow, not just in scope but in sophistication. The promise of AI—a tool to automate, yes, but more so, to enchant and engage—remains a compelling narrative in the story of modern marketing. With each advancement in AI technology, marketers are equipped to create more personalized, engaging, and effective campaigns that resonate deeply with consumers, setting the stage for a new digital marketing era where every interaction feels uniquely personal.

As we close this chapter, the narrative of AI in marketing unfolds as a symphony of innovation, with each movement—from personalization to predictive analytics—playing a crucial role in crafting compelling consumer experiences. The strategic impact of AI is not just in its ability to streamline operations but in transforming passive interactions into engaging dialogues with customers. Through practical examples and expert insights, it's clear that integrating AI is no longer just an advantage—it's necessary to remain competitive in the rapidly evolving digital landscape.

This detailed exploration of AI in marketing equips marketers with the understanding needed to harness AI effectively, ensuring that they can meet and exceed the expectations of their digitally savvy customers.

CHAPTER 5: RECENT ADVANCES IN AI MARKETING

The last year has marked an era of significant advancements in artificial intelligence (AI) within the marketing realm. Particularly, developments in natural language processing (NLP) and machine learning algorithms have transformed how brands interact with customers and predict their behaviors. These technological strides have optimized customer engagement and redefined the scope and efficacy of marketing strategies. I believe any marketeer lacking AI experts is missing the fast-moving train of development and evolution.

Technological Enhancements in NLP and Machine Learning

Natural language processing has seen notable improvements, especially with the introduction of algorithms like Google's BERT (Bidirectional Encoder Representations from Transformers). BERT has revolutionized how machines understand human language, facilitating a more nuanced interaction between consumers and digital platforms. This AI model comprehends the context of a word in a sentence rather than just the word in isolation, enabling more effective communication and relevancy in content delivery. I am not suggesting that we drop everything and rely 100% on AI, but how many of us use AI tools such as Bert, Gemini, ChatGPT, and others and find ourselves finishing tasks that used to take us weeks in less than 2 or 3 hours? Sometimes, I feel that I am talking with someone behind the screen who understands my project and my request and assists in giving the results or options that can help me decide which root I will take.

Let us dive into this Case Study: Google's BERT in Action.

One of the most illustrative examples of recent AI advancements is how Google's BERT algorithm has been leveraged in SEO and content marketing. For instance, an e-commerce company implemented BERT to enhance its product descriptions and blog content. The result was a dramatic increase in user engagement and a higher conversion rate as the content became more relevant to the consumer's queries and needs. This implementation showcases how AI's deep understanding of context can lead to tangible improvements in marketing outcomes. Understanding your customers and audience is a necessity that we can't miss, and having your assistant check everything done before utilizing your message and upgrading your action can get you moving in the right direction and, at the same time, get you closer to your target.

I've seen firsthand how BERT has shifted the SEO landscape," shares a digital marketing strategist, "And content that aligns closely with user intent because BERT understands context, not just keywords, ranks better, and engages users more deeply.

Predictive Analytics in Marketing

Alongside NLP, machine learning algorithms have profoundly advanced in predictive analytics, enabling marketers to forecast consumer behaviors with unprecedented accuracy. These algorithms analyze past consumer data to identify patterns and predict future actions. As a result, marketers can anticipate needs and tailor their strategies to meet consumer demands proactively. Dr. Helen Zhang, a renowned data scientist specializing in AI marketing solutions, emphasizes the impact of these developments: "The evolution of AI algorithms has allowed for a more nuanced understanding and anticipation of consumer needs, significantly reshaping campaign strategies." According to Dr. Zhang, these AI tools are reactive and predictive, allowing marketers to stay ahead of consumer trends and adjust their marketing efforts dynamically.

Enhanced Customer Interaction

AI's capability to improve customer interaction is not limited to predictive analytics. Chatbots, for example, have become more sophisticated thanks to advancements in AI. These bots can handle complex customer queries and provide personalized responses, enhancing customer service and engagement.

Another Case Study: AI-Powered Chatbots

A notable implementation of advanced AI chatbots can be seen in the banking sector. A leading bank introduced an AI-powered chatbot that could handle transactions, provide financial advice, and resolve customer issues through natural dialogue. This chatbot reduced the average handling time per customer interaction by 40% and improved customer satisfaction ratings due to its efficiency and accuracy. I know, don't tell me how much we sometimes suffer working with our friendly AI bank assistant, but always remember it all depends on the suitable prompts given to the chatbot and ensuring you are clear in what you are asking. Sometimes, we need human touch and experts, but chatbots can resolve some basic tasks efficiently.

AI is revolutionizing marketing by allowing us to understand customer nuances and predict their needs with greater accuracy," explains Dr. Helen

Zhang, a data scientist specializing in AI marketing solutions. "This is not just about processing data but about interpreting it intelligently and responsively."

Future Directions and Predictions

Experts predict that AI will continue to advance, particularly in emotional AI, which aims to understand and react to human emotions. This development could further personalize marketing efforts by adjusting communications based on the customer's emotional state. AI is helping marketers develop various personas that can help understand the progress of human interaction with your product and message and give you the stimulation that you need with less time and testing.

Conclusion

The recent advancements in AI have provided marketers with powerful tools to enhance personalization, predict consumer behavior, and streamline customer interactions. As AI continues to evolve, its integration into marketing strategies is expected to deepen, offering even more innovative ways to connect with and engage customers. The ongoing development of AI technologies promises to keep transforming the marketing landscape, making it an exciting time for industry professionals to explore and adopt these new capabilities.

These insights and case studies underscore the transformative power of AI in modern marketing practices, providing a comprehensive understanding of how integrating AI can lead to significant competitive advantages in the ever-evolving digital landscape.

CHAPTER 6: **WHY MARKETERS CAN'T IGNORE AI**

In the rapidly evolving marketing world, artificial intelligence (AI) is not just an advantage—it is becoming a necessity. Marketers who overlook AI's capabilities risk lagging and missing out on the strategic benefits their more AI-savvy competitors are gaining. This chapter delves into how AI reshapes the marketing landscape, drives operational efficiencies, deepens customer insights, and enhances decision-making processes. We have reached an era where we can't function properly without AI. It is not that AI replaces the human part, but it makes our lives easier and shortens the testing and research part.

The Strategic Imperative of AI in Marketing

Integrating Artificial Intelligence (AI) in marketing extends beyond simple automation. It encompasses a deep, analytical dive into vast data sets, providing insights that profoundly shape a brand's market engagement strategies. AI systems process and analyze data quickly and scale beyond human capability, uncovering patterns and delivering insights that predict consumer behavior and strategically influence marketing decisions.

AI is fundamentally designed to streamline complexity and enhance efficiency, ensuring that marketers can focus on strategy and creativity rather than mundane tasks. By leveraging various AI tools, marketing professionals can achieve higher accuracy in their campaigns and tailor their plans with a precision that traditional methods could never accomplish. Marketers must understand how to interact effectively with AI tools, ensuring they input precise prompts to obtain the desired outputs.

Dr. Ana Patel, a renowned AI expert, and author on digital transformation, emphasizes the critical role of AI in modern marketing: "AI is not just a tool; it is a transformational force that redefines the very fabric of market engagement. By automating complex processes and analyzing consumer data with unprecedented depth, AI frees marketers to focus on innovation and strategic thinking."

She continues, "To truly harness the power of AI, marketers must not only adapt to its functionalities but also become adept at steering these technologies towards achieving their business objectives. Understanding how to query AI systems effectively is as crucial as the data they process."

As AI continues to evolve, its strategic integration into marketing practices is not merely an advantage—it is imperative for staying relevant in a rapidly changing digital landscape. Marketers utilizing AI effectively will keep pace with current trends and set the stage for future innovation.

Efficiency and Cost-Effectiveness

One of the most immediate benefits of AI in marketing is its ability to enhance operational efficiency. By automating repetitive and data-intensive tasks, AI allows marketing teams to focus on strategy and creative elements. For example, AI-driven tools like Crayon utilize machine learning to track market trends and competitor activities in real time, providing brands with actionable insights far quicker than traditional research methods would allow.

Case Study: Leveraging AI for Competitive Intelligence

A prominent consumer goods company used Crayon to monitor competitive marketing moves and consumer trends. By leveraging AI to sift through vast amounts of data from social media, news sites, and competitor websites, the company could adapt its marketing strategies in real-time, significantly improving its responsiveness to market dynamics. This agility helped the company increase its market share by adapting promotions and messaging faster than the competition.

Michael Lee, Chief Marketing Officer at QuickInsights, highlights AI's transformative impact: "AI's real-time processing capabilities mean that marketers can now respond to market changes quicker than ever before, providing a significant competitive edge. This responsiveness is critical in a digital age where consumer preferences and market dynamics evolve rapidly."

Deep Customer Insights

Beyond operational efficiency, AI's ability to generate deep customer insights transforms how brands interact with their audiences. AI can create detailed customer profiles and accurately predict future behavior by analyzing data from various touchpoints.

Let us check this Case Study: AI in Personalized Marketing.

An online retailer implemented an AI system to analyze customer purchase history, online browsing behaviors, and social media activity. This comprehensive data analysis allowed the retailer to personalize marketing messages, product recommendations, and promotional offers, which led to a

30% increase in customer retention rates and a 25% increase in average order value.

The Necessity of AI for Future-Proofing

In an era where personalization and customer engagement are paramount, AI provides the essential tools for brands to stay relevant and appealing to their audiences. Ignoring AI's potential in these areas can lead to a marketing strategy that feels outdated and disconnected from the customer's needs. Always look for the right AI tools, paid or not paid, but ensure that you are testing your plan and strategy to present the work with the right insights to deliver the most significant impact. This impact will give you guidelines that can affect sales, leading to a better bottom line and better results for the business.

AI tools such as Salesforce Einstein, Adobe Sensei, and HubSpot's AI functionalities enable brands to create highly personalized experiences that meet consumers' evolving expectations. These tools can analyze customer data across multiple touchpoints, predict future behavior, and deliver highly relevant content to individual users.

Utilizing these AI tools allows companies to develop marketing strategies that are not only innovative but also directly aligned with individual preferences and behaviors, ensuring higher engagement rates and customer satisfaction. In the process, businesses can avoid the pitfalls of generic marketing approaches and establish deeper connections with their customers.

Dr. Helen Carter, an AI strategist at TechSolutions, emphasizes the importance of AI in modern marketing: "In today's digital economy, personalization is key. AI empowers marketers to tailor their offerings to individual needs and preferences, essential for building customer loyalty and driving business growth."

Conclusion

As this chapter illustrates, the use of AI in marketing is not merely a trend but a fundamental shift in how brands understand and engage their customers. Marketers who embrace AI will be well-equipped to navigate the complexities of modern consumer landscapes, while those who ignore it may be at a disadvantage. The ongoing development of AI technologies promises to continue transforming the marketing field, offering exciting opportunities for innovation and engagement.

These insights underscore the critical importance of integrating AI into marketing strategies to maintain competitive relevance and capitalize on the opportunities AI presents. The transformative power of AI in marketing is undeniable, and marketers need to harness these tools to lead in a digitally dominated future.

CHAPTER 7: **CHALLENGES & ETHICAL CONSIDERATIONS IN AI MARKETING**

Navigating the Pitfalls of AI in Marketing

While artificial intelligence (AI) presents numerous opportunities for enhancing marketing strategies, it also introduces a host of ethical considerations and challenges. These issues range from data privacy concerns to biases in AI algorithms and the overarching need for transparency in AI decision-making processes. Navigating these challenges is critical for maintaining consumer trust and ensuring the ethical deployment of AI technologies.

Data Privacy Concerns

One of the foremost ethical challenges in AI-driven marketing is the handling of consumer data. As AI systems require vast amounts of data to train and operate effectively, the potential for misuse or privacy breaches is significant. Companies like Facebook have faced scrutiny over using personal data in targeting advertisements, highlighting the delicate balance businesses must maintain. Also, we can remember what happened with Google and other social media platforms. This is a price that we have to pay to be able to get and access data that will help us formulate our plans.

"Respecting consumer privacy in AI implementations is not just about regulatory compliance; it's fundamental to maintaining trust and integrity in digital interactions," notes Dr. Emily Robertson, a data protection officer.

Case Study: Enhanced Data Privacy

Microsoft has proactively implemented robust privacy measures in its AI systems. The company employs advanced encryption and anonymization techniques to protect user data while training AI models, ensuring that personal information is not exposed or misused.

Addressing AI Bias

AI systems are only as unbiased as the data on which they are trained. Inherent biases in training data can lead to skewed or unfair outcomes, such as discriminatory pricing or targeted advertisements. Addressing these biases is crucial for fair and equitable AI applications in marketing.

Ongoing Adjustments to Mitigate Bias

Salesforce's Einstein AI platform exemplifies how continuous adjustments can mitigate biases. The platform regularly updates its algorithms to reflect diverse customer data, ensuring that all demographic groups are fairly represented. We always hunt for detailed data in every project we work on and expect the platforms to present fair and nonbiased information.

"Mitigating bias in AI is an ongoing process that requires vigilance and commitment. It's about ensuring fairness and inclusivity in all automated decisions," explains an AI ethics researcher, Sarah Connors.

The Importance of Transparency

Transparency in AI systems' decision-making processes is a crucial ethical concern, especially in marketing. Marketers are tasked with ensuring that AI applications are not opaque "black boxes." Stakeholders, including consumers, should have clear insights into how AI-driven decisions are made, particularly when these decisions impact consumer interactions and privacy.

This transparency involves disclosing the outcomes of AI decisions and explaining the underlying logic and data sources that drive these decisions. It's about opening up the algorithms for scrutiny to ensure that the AI's decision-making process can be audited and understood by those it affects. This openness helps build trust and credibility, addressing potential concerns about bias and fairness.

Incorporating Transparency Practices

To implement adequate transparency, marketers should:

1. **Disclose Data Sources:** Communicate to consumers the data being collected, the sources of this data, and how it is being used in AI models. This practice helps to ensure that users' personal information is handled responsibly.
2. **Explain Decision Frameworks:** Explain or visualize how significant decisions are made within AI systems. This could include simplified flowcharts or diagrams that explain the decision paths.

3. **Offer Opt-Out Options:** Consumers should be able to opt out of data collection or AI-driven decision processes, giving them control over their personal information.

Case Study: Enhancing Transparency

Consider a scenario where a retail company uses AI to personalize shopping experiences. By being transparent, the company can explain to its customers that their purchase history and browsing behavior data are used to recommend products. This clarity demystifies the AI process and enhances consumer trust by showing that the recommendations are not random but tailored to each user's preferences.

Professor John Kline, a prominent figure in AI ethics, emphasizes the importance of transparency: "The call for transparency in AI systems is about clarity, understanding, and accountability. Consumers have the right to know how their data is used and how decisions that affect them are made." This statement underscores companies' ethical obligation to use AI technologies transparently.

Transparency is not just a technical requirement but a fundamental element that fosters trust and accountability in AI applications. By implementing robust transparency measures, marketers can ensure that AI tools are used responsibly and ethically, aligning with broader societal values and consumer expectations. This commitment to openness will be pivotal as AI integrates deeper into various aspects of marketing and consumer engagement.

Case Study: Transparency in Practice

IBM's Watson is renowned for its transparency in decision-making processes. IBM provides detailed logs of Watson's decision pathways, allowing marketers and consumers to understand and trust how AI conclusions are drawn. In every aspect of your marketing plan or research, ensure data collection transparency is stated in your privacy statements and explanations.

Future Directions

As AI technology evolves, so does the need for robust ethical guidelines and standards. Future developments in AI will likely focus on enhancing privacy, reducing bias, and improving transparency. These efforts will be vital for AI's sustainable integration into marketing practices. I believe there will soon be guidelines to manage the world of AI that will give the audience a reason to feel at ease in their browsing or the way they use the AI platforms and tools.

Sometimes, you think AI is moving so fast that it scares you. For sure, like every tool or platform online, you will find people who are with and who are against new trends.

Conclusion

The challenges and ethical considerations associated with AI in marketing are significant, yet they are not insurmountable. By prioritizing data privacy, addressing biases, and enhancing transparency, marketers can harness the benefits of AI while upholding ethical standards and maintaining consumer trust. This careful balance will define the future trajectory of AI in marketing, ensuring that it is used responsibly and effectively.

CHAPTER 8: SKILLS MARKETER NEED TO THRIVE IN THE AI ERA

Blending Traditional Skills with AI Competency

As we navigate more profoundly into the digital age, the marketing landscape continues to evolve, requiring marketers to adapt to both time-honored practices and cutting-edge technologies. The future of marketing is not about choosing between traditional skills and new competencies but about integrating them to create more effective and efficient strategies. Proficiency in AI tools and a thorough understanding of the data that fuels these technologies are becoming as crucial as the fundamental principles of marketing.

Integrating AI with Traditional Marketing Techniques

The synergy between AI and traditional marketing techniques can create a powerful toolkit for marketers. AI's capability to analyze vast amounts of data and predict consumer behavior complements the creative and human touch that traditional marketing techniques provide. For example, while AI can efficiently segment audiences and predict what offers might interest them based on behavioral data, the human element is vital for developing creative content that emotionally resonates with consumers.

As we delve deeper into integrating AI with marketing, it's clear that a blend of traditional skills and new AI competencies is crucial for today's marketers. This chapter will explore additional case studies that highlight successful integrations of AI in marketing and provide a detailed table of essential skills for modern marketers.

Combining AI's analytical power with the human touch of traditional marketing can yield exceptional results. Here, we'll look at two case studies that exemplify this synergy:

1. **Case Study: Omni Retail Group**
    - **Challenge**: Omni Retail Group needed to improve its online customer engagement while maintaining its brand voice.
    - **Solution**: The company used AI to analyze customer data and predict buying behaviors. Marketers then used these

insights to tailor email marketing campaigns with a personal touch.
- **Result**: This approach led to a 40% increase in email open rates and a 20% uplift in conversion rates.

2. **Case Study: HealthWear Inc.**
   - **Challenge**: HealthWear Inc. struggled to effectively target customers who would benefit most from their new fitness wearables.
   - **Solution**: They could engage a more targeted audience by utilizing AI to segment their audience based on health interests and past purchase behaviors, combined with creative storytelling in their advertising.
   - **Result**: The campaign saw a 35% increase in sales for the new product line, with a significant improvement in customer feedback on ad relevance.

Case Study: Enhanced Campaign Personalization

Consider a case where a fashion retailer leverages AI to analyze purchasing trends and customer feedback. This data helps predict what new products customers might appreciate. However, the final campaign messages, which weave in emotional appeals and brand stories, are crafted by creative teams. This blend of AI-driven insights and human creativity results in a campaign that reaches the right audience and connects them personally, increasing customer engagement and sales.

Predictions and Trends: The Rise of AI-Enhanced Experiences

Looking forward, the integration of AI into marketing is set to deepen, with technologies like AI-powered voice search and virtual reality becoming more mainstream. These technologies are poised to revolutionize consumer interactions by providing more immersive and personalized experiences. The marketing world is shifting from mass communication to more personalized and direct marketing. Now, you are supposed to have multiple personas, each defining a segment of the audience, and with AI, you can understand what they are looking for. You can personalize the message to ensure the audience feels more connected with the brand. AI paved the way for more accurate messaging and better results for all the campaigns we see in the social media world. If you are not integrating AI into your planning, then you lack a clear vision for the future of your brand.

Skills Table for Modern Marketers

Here is a breakdown of the essential skills needed for marketers in the AI era:

Skill Category	Specific Skills	Importance
AI Proficiency	Data Analysis, Machine Learning	Enables precise customer segmentation and predictive analytics
Traditional Marketing	Creative Thinking, Storytelling	Essential for crafting compelling messages that resonate with audiences
Digital Proficiency	SEO, Digital Advertising	It is crucial for optimizing digital presence and engagement
Soft Skills	Communication, Problem-solving	Essential for collaboration and adapting strategies based on insights
Technical Skills	Coding (Python/R), AI Tool Mastery	Helpful in tweaking AI models and understanding algorithm outputs

A DigitalNow Consultant futurist, Tom Richards highlights these advancements' potential impact: "As voice and VR technologies improve, AI's role in creating seamless, highly personalized user experiences will become more pronounced. These technologies will enhance how we engage with consumers and require marketers to develop new skills to leverage these tools effectively."

Conclusion: Embracing AI in Marketing

"AI in marketing is more than just a tool; it's a transformative force reshaping how we understand and engage with consumers," emphasizes the critical role of AI in the future of marketing. Marketers are encouraged to embrace AI to keep up with current trends and stay ahead, ensuring their strategies remain relevant in a rapidly evolving digital landscape. This approach will enhance the effectiveness of marketing campaigns and ensure that marketers can lead the charge in innovation and customer engagement.

Marketers can unlock unprecedented opportunities and drive success in an increasingly digital world by fostering a deep understanding of traditional marketing principles and new AI technologies.

This comprehensive approach to understanding and utilizing AI in marketing is essential for modern marketers who aim to lead innovation and effectively engage with their customers. By cultivating a blend of traditional and new skills, marketers can leverage AI to create powerful, effective campaigns that drive success in the digital era.

CHAPTER 9: INTEGRATING AI WITH CUSTOMER RELATIONSHIPS MANAGEMENT (CRM)

Artificial Intelligence (AI) has become a game-changer in dynamic marketing, especially when integrated with Customer Relationship Management (CRM) systems. This fusion enhances CRM capabilities by automating interactions, personalizing communications, and predicting customer needs, fundamentally transforming how businesses engage with customers.

The Role of AI in Enhancing CRM

Integrating AI with CRM systems significantly enhances businesses' ability to effectively manage and utilize large volumes of customer data. This synergy enables companies to deliver highly personalized customer experiences at a previously unattainable scale. AI technologies can generate customized product recommendations and proactive service solutions by analyzing diverse customer data points such as behavior, purchase history, and feedback.

The effectiveness of AI-enhanced CRM systems is notably increased when there is a deep understanding of customer personas and effective communication between the AI system and the marketing team. This collaboration ensures that the insights generated by AI are actionable and align with the company's strategic marketing objectives. Fusing AI with CRM leads to more efficient data management and transforms this data into meaningful interactions that can significantly boost customer satisfaction and loyalty.

AI can help businesses anticipate customer needs, offer timely and relevant solutions, and enhance the overall customer experience. The strategic use of AI in CRM systems represents a shift from reactive customer service to a proactive customer engagement strategy, making it a critical tool for businesses looking to thrive in a competitive market.

"AI is revolutionizing CRM by transforming it from a system that merely records customer interactions to one that anticipates customer needs and engages proactively," says Dr. Linda Michaels, an expert in digital marketing technology.

Case Study: Salesforce Einstein

Salesforce Einstein is a prime example of AI integration in CRM systems. It uses machine learning to analyze data generated within the CRM to predict customer behavior, recommend the following steps, and automate routine tasks. For instance, a retail company using Salesforce Einstein observed a 25% increase in sales after implementing AI-driven insights to personalize online shopping experiences for each customer.

Personalizing Customer Communications

AI's ability to segment customers based on their behaviors and preferences is crucial for crafting personalized messages. AI-driven CRMs can trigger specific communications based on customer actions or milestones, such as sending a discount coupon on a customer's birthday or suggesting products similar to previous purchases.

Case Study: Zoho CRM

Zoho CRM integrates AI to help businesses engage customers at the right time with the right message. By analyzing past interaction data, Zoho's AI system, Zia, can predict the optimal time to contact a customer, thereby increasing the chances of message engagement and conversion. Soon, we will call our clients and tell them I am here. How can I assist you? It sounds like science fiction, but trust is not fiction anymore.

Predicting Customer Needs

Predictive analytics is another area where AI significantly boosts CRM capabilities. By forecasting future customer behaviors and needs, AI enables companies to be proactive rather than reactive. For example, AI can identify when a customer is likely to require support or is at risk of churn, allowing the company to intervene appropriately. Using AI to predict your audience's and your challenges makes the marketer's life less hectic and prepares the team to interact and deliver.

Case Study: IBM Watson

IBM Watson integrates with CRM systems to enhance customer service operations. For a telecommunications company, Watson helped predict which customers were likely to consider service upgrades based on their usage patterns and service calls. This proactive approach resulted in a higher customer retention rate and increased upsell opportunities.

Tips for Seamless AI-CRM Fusion

1. **Start with Clear Objectives**: Define what you want to achieve by integrating AI with your CRM—improving customer satisfaction, increasing sales, or enhancing personalized marketing.
2. **Ensure Data Quality**: AI's output depends heavily on the quality of the input data. Ensure your CRM data is clean, well-organized, and comprehensive.
3. **Choose the Right AI Tools**: Select AI tools that align with your CRM goals and integrate smoothly with your existing CRM software.
4. **Train Your Team**: Provide training for your marketing and sales teams on how to use AI-enhanced CRM systems effectively.
5. **Monitor and Optimize**: Continuously monitor the performance of the AI-enhanced CRM system and make adjustments as needed to optimize the results.

Examples of AI-CRM tools and platforms

AI-enhanced CRM tools and platforms offer potent capabilities for marketers leveraging advanced data analytics, machine learning, and automated communication strategies. Here are some notable AI-CRM tools and platforms that marketers can consider integrating into their strategy:

1. **Salesforce Einstein** - Salesforce's AI component, Einstein, integrates across the Salesforce Cloud platform to enhance sales, service, and marketing applications. It provides predictive analytics, natural language processing, and automated task management features to help marketers better understand customer needs and behaviors.
2. **HubSpot CRM**—Known for its user-friendly interface, HubSpot CRM integrates AI features that help with lead scoring, content optimization, and chatbot functionalities. It's beneficial for automating repetitive tasks and personalizing customer interactions at scale.
3. **Zoho CRM** - Zoho's AI assistant, Zia, offers voice and chat capabilities for sales teams to fetch information quickly. Based on previous interaction data, Zia can predict deal closures and suggest the best times to contact prospects.
4. **Microsoft Dynamics 365 AI** - This tool uses AI to provide insights and suggestions across sales and customer service modules. It helps marketers and sales professionals predict customer needs and manage relationships more effectively by analyzing data across various interaction touchpoints.
5. **Freshsales** - Freshsales features Freddy AI, which uses machine learning to effectively learn from and engage with leads and

customers. It provides predictive contact scoring, automates lead generation processes, and offers insightful sales forecasts.

These tools help manage large amounts of data and enhance interactions through personalized communication and predictive analytics, ensuring that marketers can tailor their approaches to meet their customers' evolving expectations.

Conclusion

Integrating AI with CRM is not merely a technological upgrade but a strategic necessity for businesses aiming to remain competitive in a customer-centric era. By leveraging AI, companies can transform their CRM systems from static databases into dynamic tools that anticipate customer needs and foster deeper relationships. As AI technology evolves, its integration into CRM will undoubtedly become more profound, making it an indispensable element of successful customer relationship management.

CHAPTER 10: AI AND CONSUMER BEHAVIOR ANALYSIS

In the dynamic landscape of modern marketing, Artificial Intelligence (AI) is a pivotal force in deciphering and predicting consumer behavior. This chapter delves into how AI empowers marketers to transform vast data into actionable insights, providing a deep understanding of consumer preferences and future buying habits. Once you apply the AI-CRM combination, you must understand your consumer behavior to achieve the utmost interaction result.

The Power of AI in Understanding Consumer Behaviour

AI technologies are revolutionizing the way brands understand their consumers. By employing sophisticated algorithms and data analytics, AI systems can process and analyze consumer actions, from online browsing habits to purchase history, at an unprecedented scale and speed. This analysis helps marketers to predict behaviors, tailor marketing strategies, and ultimately enhance the consumer experience.

Techniques Employed in AI Consumer Behavior Analysis

1. **Sentiment Analysis**: AI tools like Clarabridge and Brandwatch utilize natural language processing to gauge the mood and opinions expressed in social media posts, reviews, and customer feedback. This technique helps marketers understand consumer sentiments toward products or brands, which is crucial for adjusting marketing messages and strategies.
2. **Emotion AI**: Also known as affective computing, emotion AI analyses verbal and nonverbal communication to assess a consumer's mood or emotional state. Tools like Affectiva use AI to interpret micro-expressions, voice inflections, and other cues to understand better how consumers feel about marketing content, products, or services.
3. **Behaviour Prediction Algorithms**: Platforms like Adobe Experience Platform employ machine learning to predict future consumer actions based on past behaviors. This capability allows marketers to anticipate needs and personalize interactions, enhancing engagement and satisfaction.

Case Studies Showcasing AI's Impact

- **Amazon's Personalized Recommendations**: Amazon uses AI to analyze individual customer data, including past purchases, search history, and browsing patterns. This analysis powers their recommendation engine, which suggests products consumers are likely to buy, significantly boosting their conversion rates. How often do you purchase these recommendations because they are absolutely necessary? What I like is when they tell me what others bought alongside the product you ordered.
- **Starbucks' Predictive Analytics**: Starbucks employs AI to analyze the choices and preferences of its loyalty card and mobile app users. This data informs their personalized marketing campaigns and has been instrumental in increasing consumer spending by tailoring offers and recommendations to individual tastes. Starbucks knows what you are missing and craving, so why not try?

Dr. Lisa Cohen, a behavioral scientist specializing in AI, highlights the transformative impact of AI on marketing: "AI doesn't just allow us to see what consumers are doing; it helps us understand why they are doing it. By analyzing trends and patterns at a granular level, AI enables us to predict what consumers want next, sometimes even before they know it themselves."

Ethical Considerations

As AI continues to evolve, so too do the ethical considerations it raises. Concerns around privacy, consent, and the potential for AI to reinforce biases are paramount. Companies must use AI responsibly, ensuring consumer data is handled transparently and respectfully, maintaining trust and compliance with global data protection regulations.

Future Trends in AI and Consumer Behaviour Analysis

Looking ahead, AI is set to become even more integral to consumer behavior analysis. Innovations in machine learning and predictive analytics will provide even deeper insights into consumer preferences and decision-making processes. Furthermore, integrating AI with emerging technologies such as blockchain and the Internet of Things (IoT) promises to enhance data security and connectivity, opening new avenues for personalized consumer engagement.

Conclusion

AI's role in analyzing and predicting consumer behavior is undoubtedly reshaping marketing. As these technologies continue to advance, they offer marketers unprecedented capabilities to understand and meet consumers' needs. Embracing AI enhances a brand's ability to engage with its audience and solidifies its competitive edge in a market driven by personalization and consumer insights. By leveraging AI responsibly and effectively, marketers can forge deeper connections with consumers and drive future business success.

CHAPTER 11: AI-DRIVEN CONTENT STRATEGY AND SEO

In the rapidly evolving world of digital marketing, Artificial Intelligence (AI) plays a pivotal role in reshaping content strategy and search engine optimization (SEO). This chapter explores how AI tools enhance keyword research, content generation, SEO performance tracking, and the automation of content customization to align with user search intent and behavior.

AI's Influence on Keyword Research and Content Generation

AI has transformed how marketers approach keyword research, making it more data-driven and efficient. AI tools like SEMrush and Ahrefs utilize advanced algorithms to analyze search trends and user behavior, providing insights beyond basic keyword suggestions. These tools help marketers identify long-tail keywords and semantic variations, crucial for capturing niche markets and improving search visibility.

Case Study: Using Ahrefs for Market Analysis

A notable example of AI-driven keyword research can be seen with an online retailer that used Ahrefs to refine its SEO strategy. The tool's ability to analyze competitor keywords and backlink profiles enabled the retailer to identify untapped keywords and optimize their content accordingly, resulting in a 50% increase in organic traffic within six months. It is time to stop searching for the right keywords that work for your website; this tool makes it easy by giving you the correct list that effectively communicates with your audience and personas.

Automating Content Generation

Beyond keyword research, AI is revolutionizing content creation. AI-powered writing assistants like Jasper (formerly Jarvis) can generate coherent and contextually appropriate content quickly, aiding content creators in drafting articles, blog posts, and marketing copy that are both SEO-friendly and engaging.

"AI is not just automating content creation; it's enhancing the quality of content by ensuring it is highly relevant and personalized to the audience," says Emily Zhao, SEO specialist at Content Dynamics. "Tools like Jasper have become indispensable for content teams looking to scale up their content production without compromising quality."

Enhancing SEO Performance Tracking

AI also plays a crucial role in monitoring and optimizing SEO performance. Platforms like BrightEdge and MarketMuse employ AI to track content performance across various metrics, suggesting real-time adjustments for improving page rankings and user engagement.

Case Study: MarketMuse's Content Optimization

A tech company utilized MarketMuse to optimize its existing content portfolio. MarketMuse's AI analyzed the content's performance and suggested specific areas for improvement, such as depth of coverage and keyword integration. Implementing these AI-driven recommendations led to a 35% improvement in search rankings for targeted keywords.

Customizing Content to Match User Intent

One of AI's most significant contributions to SEO is its ability to tailor content to match user intent. AI systems analyze user queries to determine the underlying purpose, whether informational, navigational, or transactional, and help marketers adjust their content to meet these needs effectively. No sector can't benefit from AI integration in its marketing activities. Understanding the data is very important, and what is more crucial is being able to plan your strategy according to driven content.

Case Study: Tailoring Content with AI at Scale

A travel agency implemented an AI system to dynamically adjust its web content based on user search intent detected through AI analysis. This approach allowed them to provide more personalized content, significantly increasing user engagement and conversion rates on their travel packages.

Predictions and Future Trends

The integration of AI in content strategy and SEO is expected to grow even more sophisticated. Experts predict that AI will soon facilitate even more granular insights into user preferences and behavior patterns, enabling content to be optimized not just for search engines but for actual user engagement and satisfaction.

Conclusion

AI-driven tools are revolutionizing the field of content strategy and SEO by delivering precise, efficient, and highly effective methods for engaging with digital audiences. As these tools advance, they equip marketers with unparalleled abilities to predict user needs and devise content strategies that are both search engine-friendly and genuinely beneficial to users. Embracing AI in content strategy and SEO goes beyond merely keeping pace with tech advancements—it positions marketers at the forefront of a competitive digital marketplace. While the capabilities of AI may seem daunting due to their profound impact on predicting and influencing user behavior, when utilized with the right tools, AI can ensure that every step of your marketing campaign is meticulously planned and executed, leading to more transparent, more effective outcomes.

CHAPTER 12: **THE IMPACT OF AI ON BRAND STRATEGY**

Artificial Intelligence (AI) has become pivotal in shaping brand strategies in today's rapidly evolving marketplace. By integrating AI into their strategic frameworks, companies can refine their position in the market and revolutionize their approach to brand development and consumer engagement.

AI and Brand Audits

A brand audit is a thorough analysis of a brand's current position in the market compared to its competitors and an evaluation of its effectiveness. AI accelerates this process by analyzing large data sets about brand perception, consumer behavior, and market trends. AI systems can sift through customer reviews, social media mentions, and online content to gauge brand health and reputation more swiftly and accurately than traditional methods.

Case Study: Nike's AI-Driven Brand Audit

Nike utilizes AI to monitor brand sentiment across various digital platforms. Analyzing social media data and online reviews, AI tools help Nike identify areas where the brand's consumer perception could be improved and track how well its branding strategies resonate with the target audience. This ongoing audit allows Nike to make data-driven decisions that enhance its brand's market position.

"AI is transforming brand audits from a once-a-year event to a continual, data-driven process that helps companies stay on top of market dynamics in real-time," notes Dr. Rebecca Smith, a marketing strategist specializing in digital brand management.

AI in Competitive Analysis

AI's role in competitive analysis involves using advanced algorithms to collect and analyze data on competitors' activities. This includes tracking competitor ad spends, digital content strategies, and platform engagement. AI tools provide insights into competitors' strengths and weaknesses, helping brands adjust their approach to gain a competitive edge.

AI tools for brand audits can help companies analyze their market position, understand the brand sentiment, and track how their brand is perceived across various channels. Here are some AI tools that are particularly effective for conducting brand audits:

1. **Brandwatch** - This tool uses AI to analyze data from social media, blogs, forums, and news websites to track brand perception and consumer sentiment. It provides deep insights into how a brand is discussed online and helps identify emerging trends that could impact brand reputation.
2. **Crimson Hexagon** (now part of Brandwatch) - Known for its advanced sentiment analysis capabilities, this tool leverages AI to understand the tone and sentiment behind brand mentions across social media and other online platforms, providing detailed analytics that help brands gauge public opinion.
3. **NetBase Quid**—This platform uses natural language processing to analyze social media posts, consumer reviews, and other customer feedback forms. It provides real-time insights into brand health and consumer perceptions.
4. **Talkwalker** - Talkwalker uses AI-powered analytics to monitor, analyze, and report on brand health across social media, news, blogs, and forums. It offers features like image recognition, which can track logos and visual content related to the brand across the internet.
5. **Sprinklr** - Offers AI-driven insights to help brands listen to and engage with customers across different social media platforms. It provides comprehensive analytics that helps brands understand consumer behavior and sentiment.

These tools integrate AI technologies to provide robust analytics and insights, helping brands effectively monitor and strategize their positioning in the competitive market. These insights can help in understanding every brand's position and how to plan the next step so that you can get a higher market share and, ultimately, affect the sales of every product. Many brands are still reluctant to use AI as part of their strategies.

Example: Amazon's Competitive Analysis

Amazon leverages AI to track competitor pricing and promotional strategies in real time. This enables Amazon to adjust its prices dynamically, ensuring they remain competitive across thousands of product categories. Such AI-driven competitive analysis supports Amazon's brand positioning as a leader in market pricing and customer choice.

Dynamic Customization of Brand Messages

AI excels in customizing brand messages to different market segments or individual consumer needs by analyzing data points like past purchases, browsing behavior, and consumer demographics. This targeted approach ensures that marketing campaigns are more relevant and practical, increasing consumer engagement and brand loyalty.

Case Study: Coca-Cola's AI Personalization Campaign

Coca-Cola used AI to create personalized marketing campaigns in which vending machines enabled consumers to add their names to Coke bottles. AI analyzed purchase patterns and regional name data to predict the most popular names for customization in different areas, significantly boosting consumer engagement and emotional connection with the brand.

"AI-driven personalization isn't just about marketing efficiency; it's about creating a deeper emotional engagement with consumers," says senior digital marketing analyst Michael Zhou. "Brands that leverage AI to speak directly to individual needs and preferences are seeing substantial gains in loyalty and brand advocacy."

Conclusion

AI's impact on brand strategy is profound and far-reaching. From automating brand audits and enhancing competitive analysis to personalizing consumer interactions, AI empowers brands to navigate the complexities of modern markets more effectively. As AI technology advances, its integration into brand strategy will become more pronounced, offering even more excellent opportunities for brands to innovate and lead in their respective industries.

This chapter underscores the necessity for brands to adopt AI in their strategic planning to keep pace with technological advancements and forge ahead in creating distinctive, dynamic brand identities that resonate deeply with today's digital-savvy consumers.

CHAPTER 13: **THE FUTURE OF AI IN OMNICHANNEL MARKETING**

Artificial Intelligence (AI) is becoming a cornerstone of effective omnichannel strategies in the rapidly evolving marketing landscape. By enabling a seamless customer experience across digital and physical channels, AI enhances how brands interact with customers and revolutionizes customer engagement.

AI-Driven Content Personalization

One of the most significant contributions of AI in omnichannel marketing is its ability to personalize content across multiple platforms. AI analyses customer data from various touchpoints to tailor messages and offers that resonate with individual preferences, behaviors, and previous interactions. One of the significant aspects of the AI driver content is how they understand the users and their needs and adapt the message to fit the search history and the behavior online.

Example: Netflix's Personalization Engine

Netflix, a leader in using AI for content personalization, utilizes sophisticated algorithms to recommend movies and TV shows to users based on their viewing history and similar user preferences. This enhances user satisfaction and increases engagement across its platforms, providing a seamless experience whether users are accessing Netflix via smartphones, tablets, or smart TVs.

"Our AI-driven recommendation system is at the heart of our engagement strategy. It allows us to deliver a personalized viewing experience across multiple devices, keeping content relevant for each viewer," a Netflix product manager explains.

Customer Journey Mapping with AI

AI technologies also play a crucial role in mapping and understanding the customer journey across different channels. By collecting and analyzing data from each touchpoint, AI helps marketers identify fundamental interactions critical to the conversion process. Next, we will see how Sephora utilizes AI to increase customer satisfaction in their journey.

Example: Sephora's Cross-Channel Strategy

Sephora integrates AI to track online and in-store customer interactions, using insights to create a unified and personalized shopping experience. This strategy enables Sephora to offer tailored recommendations and promotions based on individual customer needs, enhancing the overall shopping experience.

"AI helps us bridge the gap between online and physical stores, providing a cohesive experience that our customers appreciate. By understanding each customer's journey, we can better cater to their unique beauty needs," states Sephora's marketing director.

Synchronizing Multiple Marketing Channels with AI

Effective omnichannel marketing requires not just the collection of data but also its synchronization across various channels. AI excels in integrating these diverse streams of data, enabling marketers to execute coordinated campaigns that are timely and relevant. Marketing and AI directors now understand the need to have all the technological add-ons in their plans and strategies. They integrate solutions and platforms to elevate the experience and ensure that satisfaction and journey results translate into increased sales.

Example: Home Depot's AI Integration

Home Depot uses AI to synchronize its online and offline marketing efforts, ensuring consistent promotions across every channel. Whether customers visit the website, use the mobile app, or shop in a physical store, they receive the same promotional content, reinforcing the brand's messaging and driving sales.

"AI is transforming omnichannel marketing by making it possible to collect and intelligently analyze customer data across platforms. This allows for a truly integrated marketing approach that can dynamically respond to consumer behavior," comments Dr. Angela Foster, a professor specializing in digital marketing.

The Future of AI in Omnichannel Marketing

Looking ahead, the role of AI in omnichannel marketing is set to grow even more integral. Technologies like machine learning, natural language processing, and predictive analytics will continue to advance, providing deeper insights into consumer behavior and enabling even more personalized and cohesive brand experiences.

Conclusion

As AI continues to evolve, its impact on omnichannel marketing strategies becomes increasingly profound. Companies that embrace this technology can expect to enhance their customer interactions and lead the charge in the future of digital marketing. By leveraging AI, brands can create a seamless, personalized customer journey across all channels, setting a new standard in consumer engagement.

In this chapter, we have explored how AI shapes the future of omnichannel marketing strategies, highlighting critical areas like content personalization, customer journey mapping, and the synchronization of marketing channels. As AI technology evolves, its potential to transform marketing practices offers exciting possibilities for businesses aiming to excel in a digital-first world.

CHAPTER 14: **CHALLENGES OF IMPLEMENTING AI IN SMALL TO MEDIUM ENTERPRISES (SMES)**

Adopting artificial intelligence (AI) in marketing strategies presents unique challenges and promising opportunities for small to medium enterprises (SMEs). While AI can dramatically improve efficiency, personalization, and insights, SMEs often face hurdles in resource selection and implementation strategy. This chapter explores these challenges and offers practical advice to help SMEs leverage AI effectively.

Understanding the Challenges

Resource limitation is one of the primary challenges small to medium enterprises (SMEs) face when adopting Artificial Intelligence (AI). Unlike large corporations, SMEs often operate with constrained budgets, limited access to cutting-edge technology, and smaller teams. These factors can make the initial investment in AI technologies seem particularly daunting.

Resource Constraints and AI Implementation

SMEs typically have smaller operational budgets, which may restrict their ability to invest in expensive AI solutions. Additionally, these businesses often lack the specialized personnel to develop and maintain AI systems. Team members are frequently required to wear multiple hats and may not have the time to take on complex AI projects, which can involve steep learning curves and significant time commitments.

Strategic Advice for SMEs

In situations where budget constraints and team limitations hinder AI adoption, one practical solution is to engage with third-party vendors. Outsourcing AI initiatives to external experts can alleviate pressure on internal resources, allowing SMEs to leverage AI benefits without the overhead of managing the technology directly.

Case Study: Third-Party AI Integration by a Retail SME

Consider a small online retailer that wanted to improve its customer service capabilities through AI but lacked the in-house expertise to implement a chatbot solution. The retailer partnered with a tech vendor specializing in AI-driven customer service solutions. This collaboration enabled the retailer to deploy an advanced chatbot that handled inquiries and orders, which enhanced customer satisfaction and freed up staff to focus on other critical business operations.

Expert Opinion

"Utilizing third-party AI expertise can provide a feasible pathway for SMEs to adopt advanced technologies without the need for substantial upfront investment in training and development," explains Jordan Lee, a consultant specializing in digital transformation for SMEs.

Long-term Strategy

While third-party solutions offer a good starting point, SMEs should consider gradually developing in-house AI capabilities. This approach involves training existing staff on AI technologies, possibly starting with low-code AI platforms that require less technical knowledge. More sophisticated projects can be undertaken as the team becomes more comfortable with AI tools.

Transitioning AI Tools In-House

As SMEs grow more confident in their AI capabilities, transitioning from third-party services to in-house operations can become viable. This move should be strategic, ensuring the necessary systems, infrastructure, and expertise are in place to support ongoing AI initiatives without disrupting business operations.

"AI can transform small businesses by automating tasks, enhancing customer interactions, and providing actionable insights," says Dr. Susan Martinez, a technology consultant specializing in AI solutions for SMEs. "However, the key challenge is not just adopting AI but adopting it sustainably and effectively given limited resources."

Case Study: AI Implementation in a Boutique Retailer

A boutique retailer recently integrated AI into its digital marketing strategy to enhance customer profiling and personalized communication. Despite a modest budget, the retailer partnered with an AI service provider tailored for SMEs, which allowed them to implement a cost-effective solution. The AI system helped analyze customer data and predict purchasing patterns, leading to a 20% increase in sales.

Choosing the Right AI Tools

SMEs must select appropriate AI tools that align with business needs and budget constraints. Tools like Mailchimp for automated marketing campaigns, HubSpot for CRM, and Zoho for overall business management are popular among SMEs due to their scalability and cost-effectiveness.

Practical Advice

- **Start Small**: Implement AI that addresses immediate business needs, such as automating repetitive tasks or enhancing customer service with chatbots.
- **Use Scalable Solutions**: Opt for scalable AI tools, allowing you to start with essential features and add more complex capabilities as your business grows and your budget allows.
- **Seek Expert Advice**: Consulting with AI experts or digital transformation consultants can provide insights tailored to your specific challenges and needs.

Measuring the Impact of AI

SMEs must monitor and measure AI's impact on their operations to ensure the investment delivers a sufficient return. Key performance indicators (KPIs) such as customer engagement rates, conversion rates, and overall sales growth are vital metrics to track.

Example: AI Impact on a Small Tech Company

A small tech company utilized AI to optimize its email marketing campaigns. By using AI to segment the customer base and personalize emails, the company witnessed a 30% improvement in open rates and a 15% increase in click-through rates. These metrics demonstrated the impact of AI and guided the company in refining its strategies further.

Conclusion

While integrating AI can seem challenging for SMEs, the potential benefits make it worthwhile. By starting small, choosing the right tools, and carefully measuring the impact, SMEs can overcome the challenges and reap the rewards of AI in their marketing strategies. This approach enhances operational efficiency and provides a competitive edge in the market.

Embracing AI in marketing is not merely a trend but a strategic necessity for SMEs aiming to thrive in a digital-first world. With thoughtful implementation and ongoing assessment, SMEs can successfully harness the power of AI to drive business growth and improve customer satisfaction.

CHAPTER 15: **BUILDING AI SKILLS IN MARKETING TEAMS**

Artificial Intelligence (AI) has become a cornerstone for driving innovation and efficiency. Developing AI skills within marketing teams is crucial for companies leveraging AI technologies effectively. This chapter guides training staff, creating AI-focused roles, and fostering a culture of continuous learning and innovation. It also explores AI tools that automate tasks and enhance project management. Every agency and in-house marketing department should aim to start building their list of AI tools and platforms that are a must to learn. AI should be a tool for making your marketing journey more accessible, precise, and efficient.

Training Staff in AI Skills

The first step in integrating AI into marketing strategies involves training existing personnel. This can be achieved through various programs, including online courses, workshops, and certifications from reputable institutions. Platforms like Coursera and Udacity offer specialized AI and data analytics courses tailored to marketers.

"Empowering your marketing team with AI training can transform your business outcomes," says Dr. Samantha Lee, a digital transformation expert. "It's about enhancing their capabilities to understand AI technology and apply it strategically in marketing campaigns."

Absolutely. According to Dr. Samantha Lee's perspective, integrating AI enhances a marketing team's technical capabilities and deepens their strategic insight, enabling them to devise more effective campaigns based on solid data-driven foundations.

Understanding AI and its potential outcomes allows the team and the client to set realistic expectations and recognize the value of AI-driven analytics and automation. This mutual understanding is crucial for leveraging AI to its fullest potential, ensuring that campaigns are innovative and aligned with the overarching business objectives.

Implementing AI in Marketing Campaigns

To successfully integrate AI into marketing campaigns, consider the following steps:

1. **Education and Training**: Invest in training for your marketing team to ensure they understand AI technologies and their applications within marketing. This could include online courses, workshops, or partnering with AI technology providers for specialized training.
2. **Clear Communication**: Ensure that your team and clients are on the same page regarding the use of AI. This involves clear communication about what AI can and cannot do, how it will be used in campaigns, and the expected outcomes.
3. **Choose the Right Tools**: Select AI tools that align with your marketing goals. Whether it's customer segmentation, content personalization, or predictive analytics, choosing the right tools is crucial for effective implementation.
4. **Monitor and Optimize**: Continuously monitor the performance of AI-driven campaigns and be ready to adjust. AI is not a set-it-and-forget-it solution; it requires ongoing optimization to ensure it effectively meets campaign goals.
5. **Feedback Loop**: Create a feedback loop where insights and learnings from AI implementations are regularly reviewed and integrated into future campaigns. This helps refine strategies and improve the effectiveness of AI applications over time.

By fostering an environment where AI is understood and strategically applied, marketing teams can significantly enhance their campaign planning and execution, leading to better outcomes and more robust marketing strategies.

Case Study: AI Training at a Mid-Sized Tech Company

A mid-sized technology firm implemented a comprehensive training program for its marketing team, focusing on AI and machine learning. The program included hands-on workshops and a partnership with a leading tech university. Post-training, the team successfully deployed AI-driven ad campaigns, which resulted in a 50% increase in customer engagement.

Creating New Roles Focused on AI

Integrating Artificial Intelligence (AI) in marketing revolutionizes strategy and necessitates a blend of roles that bridge traditional marketing skills with advanced AI capabilities. Creating specific roles such as AI Strategist or Data

Scientist within marketing departments is crucial for leveraging AI's full potential.

The Importance of Dedicated AI Roles in Marketing

Incorporating specialized AI roles within marketing teams ensures that expertise is available to effectively manage and optimize AI tools and strategies. These professionals act as a bridge between traditional marketing practices and cutting-edge AI applications, ensuring that AI initiatives are executed efficiently and aligned with business objectives.

Consider a scenario in a retail company where the marketing team regularly collaborates with an AI Strategist. This role oversees AI-driven projects such as customer data analysis, predictive modeling for purchasing behaviors, and personalization of marketing messages. The AI Strategist ensures that the marketing team leverages AI capabilities without siloing them from the traditional marketing processes.

AI's Role in Facilitating Cross-Departmental Collaboration

The rise of AI in marketing necessitates collaboration not just within marketing teams but across different departments, such as IT and customer service. An "IT/marketing guru" can be pivotal in ensuring that AI tools are integrated smoothly across various platforms and departments, enhancing the overall effectiveness of marketing strategies.

Case Study: Effective AI Integration at a Tech Company

A leading tech company implemented AI across its marketing strategies by appointing a dedicated AI integration specialist. This role was crucial in bridging the gap between the marketing and IT departments, ensuring that all AI tools used for marketing were in sync with the company's tech infrastructure. This strategic move resulted in a 40% increase in campaign efficiency and significantly improved customer engagement rates.

Example: AI Strategist Role at a Retail Company

A global retail brand recently introduced an AI Strategist role within their marketing team. This role focuses on integrating AI tools for customer segmentation, predictive analytics, and personalized marketing. The strategist oversees the implementation of AI technologies and collaborates with IT and data teams to optimize marketing strategies.

Fostering a Culture of Continuous Learning and Innovation

Building a culture that values continuous learning and innovation is crucial for keeping pace with AI advancements. Encouraging team members to experiment with new AI tools and techniques can lead to innovative ideas and solutions.

"Innovation in AI requires a culture that supports but drives continuous learning," comments Julia Hernandez, a renowned AI and marketing consultant. "Organizations that cultivate this culture enjoy a competitive edge by adapting more quickly to changes in technology and consumer behavior."

AI Tools for Automation and Project Management

Several AI tools can automate marketing tasks and streamline project management, allowing teams to focus on more strategic activities.

1. **HubSpot**: Integrates AI to enhance customer relationship management by predicting customer behaviors and automating email marketing campaigns.
2. **Asana**: Uses AI to optimize project management tasks, helping teams prioritize work and meet deadlines efficiently.
3. **Hootsuite Insights**: Powered by AI, it offers advanced social media monitoring and analytics, helping marketers gauge the impact of social media campaigns and refine strategies in real-time.
4. **MarketMuse**: is an AI-powered content marketing tool that automates content planning and helps optimize content for better SEO performance.

Conclusion

As marketing continues to evolve, the integration of AI will only deepen. By investing in AI skills training, creating specialized roles, and promoting a culture of innovation, companies can harness the full potential of AI to revolutionize their marketing strategies. These efforts enhance marketing teams' capabilities and drive significant business growth and customer satisfaction in an increasingly digital marketplace.

CHAPTER 16: **CASE STUDIES OF AI TRANSFORMATIONS IN VARIOUS INDUSTRIES**

Artificial Intelligence (AI) is redefining marketing strategies across various industries, from retail and healthcare to automotive and entertainment. This chapter explores several in-depth case studies illustrating how different sectors have successfully integrated AI into their marketing efforts, highlighting the transformative impact and critical lessons learned from these implementations.

Retail: Amazon's Use of AI for Personalization and Efficiency

Amazon is a prime example of AI transformation in the retail sector. The e-commerce giant uses AI to enhance customer experiences through personalized recommendations. Amazon's machine learning algorithms analyze customer data, including previous purchases, search history, and browsing patterns, to predict what products customers might like to follow. This AI-driven approach has significantly increased Amazon's conversion rates and customer satisfaction.

Quote from Amazon's AI Specialist: "Our AI systems learn from the vast amount of data we collect, allowing us to deliver a highly personalized shopping experience that customers value."

Healthcare: AI-Driven Patient Engagement by Mayo Clinic

The **Mayo Clinic** has employed AI to revolutionize patient engagement and outreach in the healthcare industry. Using AI-powered chatbots, Mayo Clinic can provide patients with timely information, answer queries, and guide them through pre-appointment processes. AI improves operational efficiency and enhances patient care by providing continuous, personalized communication.

Mayo Clinic's Digital Strategy Director says, "AI allows us to extend our care capabilities and offer personalized and accessible assistance to our patients 24/7."

Automotive: Tesla's AI Marketing Strategies

Tesla leverages AI to optimize its marketing strategies, particularly in customer segmentation and targeting. Tesla's AI systems analyze customer data from multiple touchpoints to identify potential buyers' preferences and predict which marketing messages and offers will most likely appeal to different segments. This targeted approach helps Tesla to effectively communicate the unique benefits of its electric vehicles and technology innovations.

Quote from Tesla's Marketing Executive: "With AI, we can ensure that our marketing efforts are not just broad but strikingly precise and personalized, significantly boosting our engagement rates.

Entertainment: Netflix's Content and Viewer Insights

Netflix uses AI to drive its content strategy and viewer engagement. By analyzing viewing patterns and feedback, Netflix's AI algorithms can recommend shows and movies uniquely suited to each subscriber's preferences. This approach keeps viewers engaged and informs Netflix's decisions about which new content to produce.

A Netflix Data Analyst said, "AI is at the heart of our ability to keep content compelling for each viewer, making every recommendation feel personally curated."

Lessons Learned from AI Implementations

These case studies across various industries show that while the applications of AI can vary significantly, several common lessons emerge:

1. **Data is Key**: Successful AI implementation depends on the data's quality, quantity, and relevance. Organizations must prioritize proper data management to harness AI's full potential.
2. **Customer-Centric Approach**: AI should enhance the customer experience through personalization, improved customer service, or content curation.
3. **Cross-Functional Integration**: AI's impact is maximized when integrated across various functions, from marketing and customer service to product development and operations.
4. **Ethical Considerations**: As AI technology evolves, so does the need to address ethical concerns, particularly around data privacy and the transparency of AI processes.

Conclusion

The transformative impact of AI across different sectors illustrates the versatility of AI technologies and the need for industries to adapt to these changes to remain competitive. By understanding these case studies, businesses can anticipate potential challenges and leverage AI more effectively within their marketing strategies.

AI TOOLS DISCUSSED

- **Google Analytics**: Google Analytics is a web analytics service offered by Google that tracks and reports website traffic, providing insights into user behavior, acquisition sources, and conversions. It helps marketers understand how users interact with their websites.
- **Marketo**: A comprehensive marketing automation platform owned by Adobe, designed to help businesses automate their marketing processes, manage email campaigns, and track user engagement to optimize marketing efforts.
- **IBM Watson**: IBM's AI platform offers various AI services and applications, including natural language processing, machine learning, and data analysis, to help businesses enhance decision-making and automate complex processes.
- **Jasper AI**: An AI-powered content generation tool that helps users create high-quality written content, from blog posts to ad copy, by leveraging advanced natural language processing technologies.
- **The Trade Desk**: A digital advertising platform that provides marketers with sophisticated tools to manage programmatic ad buying with real-time data-driven insights, enhancing the effectiveness and efficiency of advertising campaigns.
- **Adobe Advertising Cloud**: Part of Adobe's Digital Marketing Suite, this platform allows marketers to manage and optimize their advertising efforts across multiple channels. It provides tools for automated media buying, precise targeting, and real-time campaign adjustments.
- **Chatbot**: AI-driven software that simulates human conversation. It allows businesses to automate customer service or informational inquiries via messaging platforms, enhancing customer interaction and engagement.
- **Bert**: Bidirectional Encoder Representations from Transformers, or Bert, is a deep learning algorithm for natural language processing. It helps machines understand the nuances and context of words in searches and better interpret the intent behind queries.
- **Gemini**: Yahoo Gemini is an advertising platform that combines the benefits of search and native advertising, utilizing AI to optimize ad delivery and targeting to enhance campaign performance and user engagement.
- **ChatGPT**: Developed by OpenAI, ChatGPT is a variant of the GPT (Generative Pre-trained Transformer) architecture that is fine-tuned

for understanding and generating human-like text, enabling it to perform various language-based tasks.
- **Crayon**: Crayon is an AI-driven market and competitive intelligence platform that analyzes market trends, tracks competitors' activities, and delivers business strategic intelligence.
- **Salesforce Einstein**: Salesforce Einstein is an integrated set of AI technologies that makes the Salesforce Customer Success Platform smarter by embedding artificial intelligence into apps. This enables businesses to increase sales, improve customer service, and optimize marketing campaigns.
- **Adobe Sensei** is its artificial intelligence and machine learning framework. It powers intelligent features across all Adobe platforms and enhances capabilities in imaging, analytics, and automated marketing tasks.
- **HubSpot's AI**: Embedded within various HubSpot platforms, this AI enhances marketing, sales, and customer service operations by automating tasks like email scheduling, lead scoring, and content personalization.
- **HubSpot CRM**: This is not specifically an AI tool but a customer relationship management platform that uses AI to enhance data handling, improve customer interactions, and automate workflows.
- **Zia** is Zoho's AI assistant. It provides predictions, recommendations, and insights across the Zoho suite, helping businesses automate tasks and make data-driven decisions.
- **Microsoft Dynamics 365 AI**: A suite of AI tools integrated into Microsoft Dynamics 365 that provides insights and data-driven recommendations to enhance sales, customer service, and marketing business processes.
- **Freddy AI**: Freshworks' AI engine that enhances the capabilities of Freshdesk and Freshsales platforms by offering automated suggestions, predictive insights, and chatbot functionalities.
- **Clarabridge**: is an AI-driven customer experience management platform that analyzes text in feedback and reviews and supports interactions to derive customer sentiments and intentions.
- **Brandwatch**: a digital consumer intelligence platform that uses AI to analyze social media, the web, and other digital data to provide insights on public opinion, market trends, and consumer behavior.
- **Affectiva**: is an emotion measurement technology company that develops emotion AI, a technology used to understand human emotions based on facial expressions and voice inflections.
- **Adobe Experience Platform**: This platform provides real-time customer profiles, continuous intelligence, and automated insights into the customer journey, leveraging AI to optimize marketing efforts.

- **SEMrush**: is a powerful tool that uses AI and machine learning to provide competitive intelligence, including SEO auditing, keyword research, and online ranking data.
- **Ahrefs**: This company utilizes AI to aid in SEO and marketing tasks, providing tools for link building, keyword research, competitor analysis, and site audits.
- **BrightEdge**: An AI-driven SEO platform that helps marketers predict demand trends, understand competitors, and optimize content for maximum performance in search engines.
- **MarketMuse**: Uses AI to assist with content marketing, from planning and researching to optimization and measurement, ensuring content is targeted and effective.
- **NetBase Quid**: A consumer and market intelligence platform that provides real-time insights into customer opinions, market trends, and competitive landscapes, driven by AI analysis.
- **Talkwalker**: A social listening and analytics platform that uses AI to monitor and analyze online conversations about brands on social media, news websites, blogs, and forums.

REFERENCES

- Dr. Linda Smith says, "AI is to marketing what electricity was to the industrial revolution—an enabler of future progress that's fundamental and all-encompassing" – Page 1
- John McCarthy once stated, "As soon as it works, no one calls it AI anymore." – Page 2
- Dr. John Smith shares, "AI is akin to teaching machines to mimic the complexities of human thought. It's about crafting algorithms that can analyze, decide, and learn. Essentially, we're teaching machines how to 'think' and, importantly, learn from their 'experiences.'" – Page 3
- "The ability of AI to not just react but predict consumer needs is transforming advertising from a shot in the dark to a precision strike," asserts Maria Gonzalez – Page 6
- "AI personalization is akin to having a magical assistant who knows your customers better than they know themselves," says Dr. Emily White – Page 8
- Julia Roberts remarks, "With AI, we're not just reaching more customers, but truly connecting with them by anticipating their needs. It's like having a sixth sense for marketing." – Page 9
- Dr. Helen Zhang emphasizes the impact of these developments: "The evolution of AI algorithms has allowed for a more nuanced understanding and anticipation of consumer needs, significantly reshaping campaign strategies." – Page 12
- Dr. Ana Patel emphasizes the critical role of AI in modern marketing: "AI is not just a tool; it is a transformational force that redefines the very fabric of market engagement. By automating complex processes and analyzing consumer data with unprecedented depth, AI frees marketers to focus on innovation and strategic thinking." – Page 14
- Michael Lee highlights, "AI's real-time processing capabilities mean that marketers can respond to market changes quicker than ever, providing a significant competitive edge. This responsiveness is critical in a digital age where consumer preferences and market dynamics evolve rapidly." – Page 15
- Dr. Helen Carter emphasizes, "In today's digital economy, personalization is key. AI empowers marketers to tailor their offerings to individual needs and preferences, which is essential for building customer loyalty and driving business growth." – Page 16
- "Respecting consumer privacy in AI implementations is not just about regulatory compliance; it's fundamental to maintaining trust and integrity in digital interactions," notes Dr. Emily Robertson – Page 18

- "Mitigating bias in AI is an ongoing process that requires vigilance and commitment. It's about ensuring fairness and inclusivity in all automated decisions," explains Sarah Connors – Page 19
- Professor John Kline emphasizes the importance of transparency: "The call for transparency in AI systems is about clarity, understanding, and accountability. Consumers have the right to know how their data is being used and how decisions that affect them are made." – Page 20
- Tom Richards highlights the potential impact of these advancements: "As voice and VR technologies improve, AI's role in creating seamless, highly personalized user experiences will become more pronounced. These technologies will not only enhance how we engage with consumers but will also require marketers to develop new skills to leverage these tools effectively." – Page 24
- "AI is revolutionizing CRM by transforming it from a system that merely records customer interactions to one that anticipates customer needs and engages proactively," says Dr. Linda Michaels – Page 26
- Dr. Lisa Cohen highlights the transformative impact of AI on marketing: "AI doesn't just allow us to see what consumers are doing; it helps us understand why they are doing it. By analyzing trends and patterns at a granular level, AI enables us to predict what consumers will want next, sometimes even before they know it themselves." – Page 31
- "AI is not just automating content creation; it's enhancing the quality of content by ensuring it is highly relevant and personalized to the audience," says Emily Zhao – Page 33
- "AI is transforming brand audits from a once-a-year event to a continual, data-driven process that helps companies stay on top of market dynamics in real-time," notes Dr. Rebecca Smith – Page 36
- "AI-driven personalization isn't just about marketing efficiency; it's about creating a deeper emotional engagement with consumers," says Michael Zhou – Page 38
- "Our AI-driven recommendation system is at the heart of our engagement strategy. It allows us to deliver a personalized viewing experience across multiple devices, keeping content relevant for each viewer," a Netflix product manager explains. – Page 39
- "AI helps us bridge the gap between online and physical stores, providing a cohesive experience that our customers appreciate. By understanding each customer's journey, we can better cater to their unique beauty needs," states Sephora's marketing director. – Page 40
- "AI is transforming omnichannel marketing by making it possible to collect and intelligently analyze customer data across platforms. This allows for a truly integrated marketing approach that can dynamically

respond to consumer behavior," comments Dr. Angela Foster – Page 40
- "AI can transform small businesses by automating tasks, enhancing customer interactions, and providing actionable insights," says Dr. Susan Martinez, a technology consultant specializing in AI solutions for SMEs. "However, the key challenge is not just adopting AI but adopting it in a way that is sustainable and effective given limited resources."- Page 43
- "Empowering your marketing team with AI training can transform your business outcomes," says Dr. Samantha Lee – Page 46
- "Innovation in AI requires a culture that not only supports but also drives continuous learning," comments Julia Hernandez – Page 49

ABOUT THE AUTHOR

Born in Lebanon in 1978, the author is a proud alumnus of Notre Dame University of Beirut, where he earned a bachelor's degree in mass communication with a specialization in Radio/TV. Since starting his career in 1999, he has been a dynamic force in the agency world. With over two decades of experience, the author has driven business development, management, planning, strategy, and marketing campaigns, impacting more than 70 countries. His innovative work has won awards for best stand design and technology and set a Guinness record for a government project.

The genesis of his various books is rooted in a desire to condense years of extensive experience into actionable insights for account managers and directors, providing a practical guide through the intricacies of the fast-paced advertising industry. As a keynote speaker, the author has contributed their knowledge at numerous industry events, enhancing the professional community's understanding of marketing and business strategy. His hands-on experience in training account and sales managers ignited the spark for this book, conceived as a direct, practical resource they once wished to have.

The author is expanding their influence by working on a series of tiny pocketbooks focused on specialized topics, aiming to become a key opinion leader in his field. This book reflects their journey and is a beacon for aspiring marketers and advertising managers, guiding them toward effective leadership in their domains.

www.ingramcontent.com/pod-product-compliance
Lightning Source LLC
Chambersburg PA
CBHW050241230526
45470CB00005B/2052